For Louis Pasteur

Princeton Series of Contemporary Poets

For other books in the series, see page 66.

FOR LOUIS PASTEUR

Edgar Bowers

PRINCETON UNIVERSITY PRESS

Library of Congress Cataloging-in-Publication Data

Bowers, Edgar.
For Louis Pasteur / Edgar Bowers.
p.   cm. — (Princeton series of contemporary poets)
ISBN 0-691-06810-0 (alk. paper) — ISBN 0-691-01467-1 (pbk.)
I. Title. II. Series.
PS3503.08199F67   1989
811'.54—dc20   89-33445

Publication of this book has been aided by a grant from the Lockert
Fund of Princeton University Press

This book has been composed in Linotron Bembo

Clothbound editions of Princeton University Press books are
printed on acid-free paper, and binding materials are chosen for
strength and durability. Paperbacks, although satisfactory for personal
collections, are not usually suitable for library rebinding

Printed in the United States of America
by Princeton University Press
Princeton, New Jersey

Contents

II

III

Acknowledgments

Poems in this volume have appeared in the following publications:

The Threepenny Review
The Southern Review
Raritan
Drastic Measures
Walking the Line (R. L. Barth)
Numbers
Poetry Nation Review
Poetry Durham

I

For Louis Pasteur

"Who is Apollo?"—College student

How shall a generation know its story
If it will know no other? When, among
The scoffers at the Institute, Pasteur
Heard one deny the cause of child-birth fever,
Indignantly he drew upon the blackboard,
For all to see, the Streptococcus chain.
His mind was like Odysseus and Plato
Exploring a new cosmos in the old
As if he wrote a poem—his enemy
Suffering, disease and death, the battleground
His introspection. "Science and peace," he said,
"Will win out over ignorance and war,"
But then, the virus mutant in his vein,
"Death to the Prussian!" and "revenge, revenge!"

How shall my generation tell its story?
Their fathers jobless, boys for the CCC
And NYA, the future like a stairwell
To floors without a window or a door
And then the army: bayonet drill and foxhole;
Bombing to rubble cities with textbook names
Later to bulldoze streets for; their green bodies
Drowned in the greener surfs of rumored France.
My childhood friend, George Humphreys, whom I still see
Still ten years old, his uncombed hair and grin
Moment by moment in the Hürtgen dark
Until the one step full in the sniper's sight,
His pastor father emptied by the grief.
Clark Harrison, at nineteen a survivor,
Never to walk or have a child or be
A senator or governor. Herr Wegner,
Who led his little troop, their standards high
And sabers drawn, against a panzer corps,
Emerging from among the shades at Dachau

Stacked like firewood for someone else to burn;
And Gerd Radomski, listening to broadcasts
Of names, a yearlong babel of the missing,
To find his wife and children. Then they came home,
Near middle age at twenty-two, to find
A new reunion of the church and state,
Cynical Constantines who need no name,
Domestic tranquility beaten to a sword,
Sons wasted by another lie in Asia
Or Strangeloves they had feared that August day;
And they like runners, stung, behind a flag,
Running within a circle, bereft of joy.

Hearing of the disaster at Sedan
And the retreat worse than the one from Moscow,
Their son among the missing or the dead,
Pasteur and his wife Mary hired a carriage
And, traveling to the east where he might try
His way to Paris, stopping to ask each youth
And comfort every orphan of the state's
Irascibility, found him at last
And, unsurprised, embraced and took him in.
Two wars later, the Prussian, once again
The son of Mars, in Paris, Joseph Meister—
The first boy cured of rabies, now the keeper
Of Pasteur's mausoleum—when commanded
To open it for them, though over seventy,
Lest he betray the master, took his life.

I like to think of Pasteur in Elysium
Beneath the sunny palm of ripe Provence
Tenderly raising black sheep, butterflies,
Silkworms and a new culture, for delight,
Teaching his daughter to use a microscope
And musing through a wonder—sacred passion,
Practice and metaphysic all the same.
And, each year, honor three births: Valéry,
Humbling his pride by trying to write well,

Mozart, who lives still, keeping my attention
Repeatedly outside the reach of pride,
And him whose mark I witness as a trust.
Others he saves but could not save himself—
Socrates, Galen, Hippocrates—the spirit
Fastened by love upon the human cross.

THIRTEEN VIEWS OF
SANTA BARBARA

Hang Gliding

When hang gliders wait for the wind, they wait
Together in a row. The mountain light
Recalls the young man from his solitude.
Then, leaping out from off the farthest ridge,
Will open to the wind's will, over his
Lone shadow's long companionship, he rides
His valor's widening circles toward the city—
Tile roofs, white buildings, playgrounds, streets and
  gardens.
The sun extends its arm. The islands lie
A bony shadow grasping wave and cloud.
The cold twin hunts beneath the southern tree.

Air, water, places and the missing People,
A memory older than Prometheus,
The long deep boat, the basket's true design,
The suffering hand and eye. In the western sky
A rocket unweaves the tapestry of Cronos.
Black dolphins arch their backs on the dying sea.
The blood-cursed Mission minds the spinning year
While, through the pass the Fathers call Saint Mark,
Fremont's Yankees steal on the town below.

I was a gliderman. By the North Sea
Each winter dusk, we watched the gathering host
Shape like a darker wing its ritual:
Cologne's twelve temples, Düsseldorf's iron bridge,
Dresden's theaters—the Melian nemesis.
Then back at dawn, lights blinking, one by one.
There is a hill near Cambridge where the sons
Their fathers buried lie before a wall,
On its smooth order, a strict account, the names
Of airmen and of seamen yet unburied,
Brief lesser stars across a zodiac.

Mask of the Dan Tribe, Ivory Coast

Over the study-table hangs a mask,
Feathers for hair and copper slits for eyes,
Lips parted, cheekbones tight and nostrils flared—
The maker's introspection for his tribe.
The chain of being is its daily bread.
Sub-zero cold and heat that seems a cloud
Where spirits of a spirit rest or move
Contain its time. Serpent, lion and eagle
Are language for its empty mouth to tell.
The passion of its gaze is like the seal
Playing among the surfers in the surf
Or one kite in the storm cloud, tugging hard.

The Hill

Sometimes we watch the sunset from a hill
In front of Josten's, maker of cups and bowls
As prizes for young swimmers, runners and rowers.
The freeway, the old snake of many eyes,
Divides the darkened oak trees from the beach.
The sky is red, the sea its other self.
And I remember Ajax, that he came,
Spent by the stupid cunning and bought vote,
To sink, as his last deed, on his true friend.
Around the cove, a house, the small tough hope,
The sail that braved the Cape and claimed the bay.

The Beach

In spring, we fish for halibut. In summer,
When grunion spawn at midnight in the surf,
We look for them on the sand to throw them back.
In winter, from the point, we cast beyond
The breakers to where the bass feed. Solar age
And mythic distance turn round the point's ellipse.
Earth is dark. Air darkens. The moon is white.
Then, as if I were there, I watch us here,
Immensities of purpose barely visible
Intent upon the message in the line
Startlingly taut with sudden gravity,
Muscle and bone of the reflected light.

The Botanic Gardens

Poppies bloom in the meadow below the mountain,
And, in the bare light, by the bare walks, each
A soul distinct and modest, all of one
Order between the namer and the name,
Grow trees and shrubs and flowers that love the coast.
Under the hill, set high above the flood,
A dam, filled to the lip with sand, a race
To the Mission, primitive, dry in leaves—
As if another walks there! As if walk,
Through fledgling sycamores, the voiceless noon
And storied ocean, while the years to come
Circle each trunk with rain or lack of rain.

The Resident

Young, she went East to school, was married, reared
Two sons and, when her husband died, returned.
Old oaks, like Buddhas, touch her father's ground;
Navajo rugs, library, a wing for guests;
Quiet, her mother's chapel, its stained glass;
A Japanese dog for company, poise and charm.
Now, from a wheelchair, she is gathered in,
Sister, son, wife and child learning the way.
Outside of Oxford, driving a rented Saab,
She rubbed a car too narrow in the lane,
Whose owner, wrathful, blamed her. She blamed him.
Indignant, "It is my country." "All the more
Reason to be a gentleman," she said.

The Vedanta Temple

From England to New England once they sailed,
The Anabaptist brothers, to discover
The holy city promised them. Their sons
Grew with the maple trees. Slow fires in spring
Gave incense to the passion of their hardship
And wine enough for tables high and green.
After Ticonderoga, set adrift
In wagons covered over by a sail,
They came to farm in Iowa and suffered
Their sons' slow death in deltas far away.
Another voice revealing a parentage
Of time repeating futures endlessly,
Past cities lost in colors of the sun
And forests of saguaro, past the lake
Saltier than the tide, they came at last
Through mountains to the floor of vanished seas;
Raised apricots, figs and grapes, melons and apples;
Built and launched ships to bear their sons as far
As Iwo Jima, Hiroshima, Nagasaki.
Now, in their time, released to the voice within
And faithful to the Sabbath, they have come,
Beyond the crude novitiate's bare wall,
The Greek farm house, grey olive and black acacia,
To the Vedanta temple, as to a ship
At rest on a higher, dryer wave, the still,
Slow, spicy air, Connecticut or Vermont.

The Campus

After a class in the new building, nearer
The slough where egrets pause in their flight south—
Long halls, blind doors, dark stairs—walking to lunch
Past Music, Art, Psychology and Drama,
We stop to watch the rabbits: the dark eye,
The knowing ears and nose, the soft decorum
Ancestral and inhuman. And we, all silent,
Amazed and joyful for our want of skill.

Little brothers, one thousand generations
Lived here forever as in a living shell:
Lime-life, fin-life and wing-life, eye, mouth and hand
Within the cardinal virtues of the sky.
Sons of Saint Francis brought them each a soul,
And, in four generations, all were gone;
Their elegy, the dance of mist and light.
Then, where a few gulls cry, some hasty barracks,
Hasty roads and hasty gun-emplacements
Marked now by tide's advance and tide's retreat.
How shall the promise feel its consequence!
The full cup overfill its lip with sand!

On these pale souls and on these children's children,
Saint Francis and Saint Socrates, have mercy.

El Camino Cielo

In the mountains, Sundays and holidays, they shoot
At bottles, cans and cardboard targets, clinging
To rifles as if to slot machines. Perhaps
They summon up the genie that denies
Unhappiness as a mystery of fate,
As absolute, the punishments of time.
Neighbor and neighbor's son, perhaps they envy
The satisfaction of the golden eagle
Over the lake, teaching its young to fly,
Or feel *contemptus mundi* for the rattler
Tasting the ricochet on its quick tongue
Or for the sacred hunt in painted caves.
They leave behind them weather's emeralds
Among the marks of fury, scarred and scattered.

The Visitor

The January warmth reminded him
Of winters in Montana. Idling the beach,
Pelicans' sudden dive through a rabble of gulls,
He listened to the trains for Summerland
Reminding him again of boyish trains
He might have taken, his people, who laid the track,
And great plains, tragic, surprised by August hail.
These things he wrote of, nights, his firm heart beat
Ironic with odd and even, the play of surf,
Venus and Mars. Later, silent TV,
Old movies for the old harsh intimacy.

Mornings, with his uncareless gait, he ventured
Round foreign car and winter bloom to where
Young men and old men practice the Christian life:
Nautilus, sauna, jacuzzi, swim and shower.
And wandered back through Bonnymede, big house
Awry and empty, lemon grove heaped for a pyre,
Wind sock alert for a ghost plane. From the mound
The People kept their dead in, watching the fine
Bodies defy the fault-line in the wave
Arched high and cold, he proposed an epitaph:
No shame, no terror and no day of wrath.

Davey Brown Camp

Camping, around the fire at night, we sing
Songs our mothers taught us or songs we sang
At summer camp, in church or in the army;
Then, from our sleeping bags, we name the stars.
All afternoon, quietly among the pines
That open their cones only in fire, we followed
The soar of condors down the loop of time.
Breakfast over, we climb the wilderness,
Hoping to see a lion on the fire road
And it see us before it slips away.

The Museum of Natural History

The small museum is a labyrinth.
In light or darkness, Waldo Abbott's birds,
Species complete in every feathered one,
Changelessly imitate their little time.
Somewhere unknown, young Horus on the wing,
His wind the light, his light a space, his space
A measurement triangular and sure,
Excites the wondering eye that looks for him.
And, at the entrance, leviathan awaits
Exodus to the promised deeper sea.

The Courthouse

On the walls around Napoleon are depicted
His true remains. These studied images,
Civic narrations and expectancies,
Move those who go to wonder at his tomb
Like shapes that move through water as a wave.

Our Moorish-Latin courthouse! Murals bring
Cabrillo shoreward. Junípero Serra's flock
Watch blind desire apportion earth and sea
On scales of gold. Green tree and kingly ranch
Spread from imperial oil to the western gate:

Acres of flowers for seed; nearby, dry fields
For blast-off, for failure and failed ambition
Past intimate horizon to the far.
We who had sought the symbols of the spirit
To have life more abundantly, discoverers

From spirit's old anxiety, explore
The courtrooms like a logic, for a premise,
Uneasy before the flags and photographs
Of boys who traveled east to fight a war
With other boys equally free and brave.

The Radiologist

Surrogate eye a mind like mine has made,
Extension of the self to know the self,
Looks at the Me that, drunk on its own dust,
The Martian archeologist may find;
Or, with a smaller brain, explores the dark
Folded below the stomach like a root,
Root of the eye that only looks without.

Aristocrat of time, the eye that proves
Transparence and remembers it as speech
Mine pictures as a youthful orange grove,
Intensity of being, in a place,
That stores in bitter fruit what he may find
And taste of, though it be a time's translation
And "Doctor, know thyself" its *areté*.

Epilogue: The Yacht

High winds have pushed the little yacht adrift.
It lies alone, stranded against the sand,
No whale or dolphin to sport with, breeze to play with.

Back to the harbor, where, dreaming a summer calm,
Its comrades lie, half-asleep on the sullen tide,
Wanders its simple ghost and calls to them:

"Comrades, our time is short, our summers few,
Our joys soon over. Try, while you may, the far
Wave sumptuously beneath the golden eye,

Your white hull in blue pastures off Peru;
Or dare the iceberg free of the creeping glacier
While there are stars to guide you safely through."

O earth and sea, pity its small regret.
If an unchanging summer keeps a harbor,
Step lightly, earth, and sea, speak quietly.

WITNESSES

Adam

The shadowtail, the cottontail, the jay,
The spider on her trembling web, the mote
Swimming my blood—all innocent, all true,
All unsuspecting! But someone was there.
The burden of the past and future, father
And child of choice, he offers count and name.
It is as though, beneath a foreign tree,
Gifted with tongues, familiar of the brute,
I made a garden, kissed a face and died.
Children I might have had, remember me,
That, in your quiet house, your word emerge.

Eve

I wonder if the Lord who walked the earth
And spoke to us could be the thought I had
When, by the pool, I watched your face and thought
The whole creation filled by what I saw;
Or he could be the dream—parent of thought,
Substance and the exchange of substance—that,
As what will be would be like what has been,
So love, this vulnerability, this gift,
Should be the fate we chose, that our hope stay
And children of that dream remember us.

Cain

I thought my death, divided past from future:
It was as if the face in the mirror changed,
As if the light were father, brother, son,
But darkened, and the darkness were a science
And I the scientist. It is as if
That absence, where the generations seek
A presence, were the first science! My twin,
Your perfect candor waits in memory's cave.
We two shall be a one where none has gone.

Noah

Older, I count the fantasy of life,
The stories, persons, disappearances
That were or might have been. Beyond myself,
Complete in being, impersonal as name,
They are my book. I enter into print!
I hear the sound of ever-moving water
Repeated as the formal, true, exact
Inconsequential consequence of time,
The city and the savage in the long
Mysterious unredemption of desire.
Now, in distress, shall I assume a story—
Hermes, who leaves me here, and vanishes?
Or speak of how the dove, the messenger,
Flies from the mortal hand to seek its way?

Jacob

In tangled vine and branch, high weed and scrub,
I found a tree my father planted once,
A thread-leaf maple, green and old, not tall
As I am tall, but ten-foot at the base—
Ten thousand leaves contained as of one leaf.
As though I lay, wrapped in the ancestral root,
Head on the stone, awake in sleep, I knew
The unity in which earth walks the earth,
Struggles with speech until a name is said,
Is lamed and blessed. A cloudless summer day.
Years up the ladder of the sky, beyond
Air, fire and water, a jet plane barely moved,
Marked on the blue as on the final stone—
Feather, leaf, shell, fish-print or whitened bone.

II

On Dick Davis' Reading,
California State University, Los Angeles

While Dick reads, looking up, he sees the quiet
Attention of his listeners, like a voice
Within a body eager for its health;
And in his voice made larger by the meter,
As on a low relief laid on the shield
Hephaestus makes the hero, they can see
The gods again, immortal in the error
Disfiguring and busying the world.
Earlier, along the choleric tense freeway,
Apollo's torso, alien and severe,
Seen for a moment, surprised him. There, on a frieze
Of pediments and columns falling in pieces
Below tall buildings walking half-asleep,
The calm look seemed the rhythm meant for him
Over the car's dull resonant momentum.
His voice recalls the spirit to its story,
The spirit whose listening crowds the crowded room—
Quiet, a bow taut to the feathered shaft—
These heirs of Achilles' bitter day at school,
First pupil of the first Academy.

On Edmund Wrobleski's Concern for His Patient

Handsome and young, his smile almost a schoolboy's,
Edmund Wrobleski, after a day of rounds,
Emergencies and visits, late toward evening
Examines his oldest patient's heart and sees,
Because of the disorder he can hear,
Still, in his psyche bright with meditation,
The firm new apple shining on the tree
And, rising from the flow and ebb of time,
Old youth and beauty. Therefore, when he smiles,
It is because in that oblivion
Each new apparel, human or divine,
Shines like an icon, his faithful meditation—
Though rose and white and gold be lost to ash
And grey seem the first principle—still present
At Epidaurus for the festival
Of Aesculapius and the tragic muse.

On Clive Wilmer's Visit to the Wildfowl Refuge

Come winter's night and icy dawn, like hunters,
Clive and Gabriel, his thirteen year old son—
Clive with his copper beard and Saxon eyes,
Gabriel with his Celtic hair and skin—
At Welney, on the Roman fen, await
The swans from Iceland. At California Valley
On the Carrizo Plain, we later pilgrims
Are up before the sun to watch the cranes.
The honor and the dignity of ghosts
Exalt their flight and solemnize its shape.
We feel the one great circle to the Poles.

As quietly as ghosts, the swans appear,
White acolytes afloat on blue and gold,
Long-suffering, mild, archaic saurians
Escaped from a Death Valley of the past
Where no grouse crouches pale beside a stone,
Turns its eggs every day, then, in its feathers,
Brings water to its chicks. I know a man,
John Lamb, who thinks his father, dead sixty years,
Still cares for him and, like a saint, still keeps
Benign attendance on his longer journey.
And the six basic particles of matter
Have waited patiently for someone's mind
To know themselves and, as they know, are like
A constellation lifted through the dark.

The swans within his glasses, Gabriel
Feels the discomfort of Eros at his shoulders
And, wondering that he seems to hear the sea lions
And dolphins at their play in dens and forests,
Their trial soon over, Mars an angry fist
Of drought and heat where nothing lives or dies,

Imagines life just like the Roman tales
He reads at school, where change is spirit's art
And rituals of change its permanence,
His *vita brevis* long as they are long.

Richard

The space between his parents and his bed
Seems a thick dull plastic, the San Diego
Newspaper and the flowers they brought grey wax.
By their inaudible cries of helpless love
Bewildered and annoyed, intent upon
The cancer in his lung, he looks instead
On time's cold hardening surface for the child
Complicit with his fate; or, still a child,
Envies the nurse his lucky hour downtown
With other sailors. Then he remembers how,
Alone all night with his mortality,
Far from the tightening circle and the window,
The city and the ships in port, he flew
Across the wide Pacific to his berth.
There, from the hovering helicopter's spirit
Let down by a chain of gold, blue ensigns snapping,
Amid shrill pipes the brilliant summer crew,
The wet deck heaving in the storm, he hears,
Over his rapt salute, the young Chief Engineer's
"Welcome aboard, lieutenant" to his appointed years.

Thomas

A porter found him in the Pullman car,
A few weeks old, dressed like a rich man's child.
The orphanage named him Thomas, for Aquinas.
The parents who adopted him were Czech,
New immigrants, the promise of the new
Betrayed by the Depression, the greying city
Idle, but for Feller on the mound
And Fred and Ginger's pastorals on the screen.
At school he read his namesake, then, in the Air Force,
As if a revelation sent to him,
His lineage and his birthright. Their starry son,
Trying untried elations of the skies
Above the green earth's curve, his silver wing
Climbing and spinning through undarkened day,
He grasped the golden bowl and drank the wine,
His pride and joy like Hermes' beauty, wings
Dancing with every debutante, a feast
Of arms for boys and girls, where no death is.
The destiny that holds the hero's life
Appeared to him above the clouds of France
In combat, on the field of dread. Messerschmitts
Everywhere in pursuit of his pursuit,
He never reported sick or turned away
Suddenly over the Channel, for a year,
Till over Frankfurt screaming from its pyre,
Engine aflame, then cockpit, he bailed out,
The parachute his spirit in the dark.
Burnt air, burnt earth, burnt time! An angry mob
Mistook him for another bomber pilot
And hanged him from a tree, near Goethe's house.

Mary

The angel of self-discipline, her guardian
Since she first knew and had to go away
From home that spring to have her child with strangers,
Sustained her, till the vanished boy next door
And her ordeal seemed fiction, and the true
Her mother's firm insistence she was the mother
And the neighbors' acquiescence. So she taught school,
Walking a mile each way to ride the street car—
First books of the *Aeneid* known by heart,
French, and the French Club Wednesday afternoon;
Then summer replacement typist in an office,
Her sister's family moving in with them,
Depression years and she the only earner.
Saturday, football game and opera broadcasts,
Sunday, staying at home to wash her hair,
The Business Women's Circle Monday night,
And, for a treat, birthdays and holidays,
Nelson Eddy and Jeanette McDonald.
The young blond sister long since gone to college,
Nephew and nieces gone, her mother dead,
Instead of Caesar, having to teach First Aid,
The students rowdy, she retired. The rent
For the empty rooms she gave to Thornwell Orphanage,
Unwed Mothers, Temperance and Foster Parents
And never bought the car she meant to buy;
Too blind at last to do much more than sit
All day in the antique glider on the porch
Listening to cars pass up and down the street.
Each summer, on the grass behind the house—
Cape jasmine, with its scent of August nights
Humid and warm, the soft magnolia bloom
Marked lightly by a slow brown stain—she spread,
For airing, the same small intense collection,
Concert programs, worn trophies, years of yearbooks,
Letters from schoolgirl chums, bracelets of hair

And the same picture: black hair in a bun,
Puzzled eyes in an oval face as young
Or old as innocence, skirt to the ground
And, seated on the high school steps, the class,
The ones to whom she would have said, "*Seigneur,
Donnez-nous la force de supporter
La peine,*" as an example easy to remember,
Formal imperative, object first person plural.

Elegy: Walking the Line

Every month or so, Sundays, we walked the line,
The limit and the boundary. Past the sweet gum
Superb above the cabin, along the wall—
Stones gathered from the level field nearby
When first we cleared it. (Angry bumblebees
Stung the two mules. They kicked. Thirteen, I ran.)
And then the field: thread-leaf maple, deciduous
Magnolia, hybrid broom and, further down,
In light shade, one Franklinia Alatamaha
In solstice bloom, all white, most graciously.
On the sunnier slope, the wild plums that my mother
Later would make preserves of, to give to friends
Or sell, in autumn, with the foxgrape, quince,
Elderberry and muscadine. Around
The granite overhang, moist den of foxes;
Gradually up a long hill, high in pine,
Park-like, years of dry needles on the ground,
And dogwood, slopes the settlers terraced; pine
We cut at Christmas, berries, hollies, anise
And cones for sale in Mister Haymore's yard
In town, below the Courthouse Square. James Haymore,
One of the two good teachers at Boys' High,
Ironic and demanding, chemistry;
Mary Lou Culver taught us English: essays,
Plot summaries, outlines, meters, kinds of clauses
(Noun, adjective and adverb, five at a time),
Written each day and then revised, and she
Up half the night to read them once again
Through her pince-nez, under a single lamp.
Across the road, on a steeper hill, the settlers
Set a house, unpainted, the porch fallen in,
The road a red clay strip without a bridge,
A shallow stream that liked to overflow.
Oliver Brand's mules pulled our station wagon
Out of the gluey mire, earth's rust. Then, here

And there, back from the road, the specimen
Shrubs and small trees my father planted, some
Taller than we were, some in bloom, some berried
And some we still brought water to. We always
Paused at the weed-filled hole beside the beech
That, one year, brought forth beech nuts by the thousands,
A hole still reminiscent of the man
Chewing tobacco in among his whiskers
My father happened on, who, discovered, told
Of dreaming he should dig there for the gold
And promised to give half of what he found.

During the wars with Germany and Japan,
Descendents of the settlers, of Oliver Brand
And of that man built Flying Fortresses
For Lockheed, in Atlanta; now they build
Brick mansions in the woods they left, with lawns
To paved and lighted streets, azaleas, camellias
Blooming among the pines and tulip trees—
Mercedes Benz and Cadillac Republicans.
There was another stream further along
Divided through a marsh, lined by the fence
We stretched to posts with Mister Garner's help
The time he needed cash for his son's bail
And offered all his place. A noble spring
Under the oak root cooled his milk and butter.
He called me "honey," working with us there
(My father bought three acres as a gift),
His wife pale, hair a country orange, voice
Uncanny, like a ghost's, through the open door
Behind her, chickens scratching on the floor.
Barred Rocks, our chickens; one, a rooster, splendid
Silver and grey, red comb and long sharp spurs,
Once chased Aunt Jennie as far as the daphne bed
The two big king snakes were familiars of.
My father's dog would challenge him sometimes
To laughter and applause. Once, in Stone Mountain,
Travelers, stopped for gas, drove off with Smokey;

Angrily, grievingly, leaving his work, my father
Traced the car and found them way far south,
Had them arrested and, bringing Smokey home,
Was proud as Sherlock Holmes, and happier.
Above the spring, my sister's cats, black Amy,
Grey Junior, down to meet us. The rose trees,
Domestic, Asiatic, my father's favorites,
The bridge, marauding dragonflies, the bullfrog,
Camellias cracked and blackened by the freeze,
Bay tree, mimosa, mountain laurel, apple,
Monkey pine twenty feet high, banana shrub,
The owls' tall pine curved like a flattened S,
The pump house Mort and I built block by block,
Smooth concrete floor, roof pale aluminum
Half-covered by a clematis, the pump
Thirty feet down the mountain's granite foot.

Mort was the hired man sent to us by Fortune,
Childlike enough to lead us. He brought home,
Although he could not even drive a tractor,
Cheated, a worthless car, which we returned.
When, at the trial to garnishee his wages,
Frank Guess, the judge, Grandmother's longtime neighbor
Whose children my mother taught in Cradle Roll,
Heard Mort's examination, he broke in
As if in disbelief on the bank's attorneys:
"Gentlemen, must we continue this charade?"
Finally, past the compost heap, the garden,
Tomatoes and sweet corn for succotash,
Okra for frying, Kentucky Wonders, limas,
Cucumbers, squashes, leeks heaped round with soil,
Lavender, dill, parsley and rosemary,
Tithonia and zinnias between the rows;
The greenhouse by the rock wall, used for cuttings
In late spring, frames to grow them strong for planting
Through winter into summer. Early one morning
Mort called out, lying helpless by the bridge.
His ashes we let drift where the magnolia

We planted as a stem divides the path.
The others lie, too young, at Silver Hill,
Except my mother. Ninety-five, she lives
Three thousand miles away, beside the bare
Pacific, in rooms that overlook the Mission,
The Riviera and the silver range
La Cumbre east. Magnolia grandiflora
And one druidic live oak guard the view.
Proudly around the walls, she shows her paintings
Of twenty years ago: the great oak's arm
Extended, Zeuslike, straight and strong, wisteria
Tangled among the branches, amaryllis
Around the base; her cat, UC, at ease
In marigolds; the weeping cherry, pink
And white arms like a blessing to the blue
Bird feeder Mort made; cabin, scarlet sweet gum
Superb when tribes migrated north and south.
Alert, still quick of speech, a little blind,
Active, ready for laughter, open to fear,
Pity and wonder that such things may be,
Some Sundays, I think, she must walk the line,
Aunt Jennie, too, if she were still alive,
And Eleanor, whose story is untold,
Their presences like muses, prompting me
In my small study, all listening to the sea,
All of one mind, the true posterity.

III

On Robert Wells' Moving from Tours to Blois

To honor the discovery of the soul,
Roy Bundy and I sometimes played the game
Of choosing what new psyche we would take
Upward along the scale of transmigration.
His preference was the Rocky Mountain sheep,
True Pindarist, alert from rock to ledge
And ledge to cliff face, the patrician balance,
Heroic generosity and pride
Watching us from a granite photograph
By Phidias and Michelangelo.
I never could decide between the eagle
In skies above Tiepolo's delights,
Pieties and grave airy enthusiasm,
And, grown wise in the trees of good and evil,
Its blood a liquid sunshine, menacing
The monkeys of Douanier Rousseau,
The anaconda. Robert, since you choose
To move with your Marie Christine to Blois,
You chose the salamander, the Pythian flame
In fresh clear frequencies of rock and pool
As civil as a tapestry. How wise
Theocritus and Virgil's choosing you
For their new soul! Now, since Marie Christine
Teaches and heals the body, there, together,
You two are that elation of the self
Claude paints with, in the colors of the Claude
Monet we also love. Then, farewell, prairies,
Where rabbits sport all midnight in the ghostly
Pale orange glare of street lights outside Tours!
They might be some of my late students, someday
Perhaps as alive as Dürer's lithograph,
Expressions added later by Kilroy
Or someone even more anonymous.

The Devereux Slough

I have read that for Descartes all things alive
Or not alive are solid void, except
Equations. So these ducks, green bill and head,
Are graphs on blanks of subjectivity,
Their quacks some numbers searching for an ear
Itself a motion thin as light. And since
All void is gravity, it obligates
The farthest fleeing cluster to their flight,
The light year to their anniversary,
The measured naught, the measure variation.
Our cosmic Heraclitus never rests!

Behold this book between us on our knees,
The idiosyncratic pictures, the descriptions
Of how, from pools reflective of the skies
And clouds in Manitoba, the memory
Of this slough like a pinpoint on a map
Is expert navigation by the stars;
Of Chanticleer and Pertelote, design
Symmetrically precise, colors repeated
As formally as their migration's course—
Behavior for the Muses! As before,
You read to me of warmer, richer waters
Along my thought's equator, where they swim
Until the season to look for them again.

Behind us is the school for children who
In letters cannot find their way, who read
The *b* before the *a*. Listen to them
Laugh when the snowy egret from its perch
In bushes by the shore suddenly rises.
The fear and greed of the ducks! The children
Run crying on the sand to where the wave beats.
In the pale winter day the hills are pale

Shades of more color than there is alphabet.
By such excitements moved to say I love you,
I know from both our doubts how much the greater
Certitude shall require the more illusion.

A Meditation on "The Devereux Slough"

First, you imagine a teacher, a young
Woman with dark brown hair, black eyes, and skin
White as Iseult's or as an old French rose,
Her voice precise and modest, her gesture quiet,
And, since clothes are essential to a Self,
Blue cashmere sweater over a yellow dress.
There will be more detail, of course, as you
Remember the young women you have known.

Then imagine her students, thirty-five
Of California's best, not Jacks and Jills
But Jennifer and Carlos, every one
Precious for the particulars you find;
So take your time, the class lasts fifty minutes.
Imagine Carlos as a Dane or Swede
(With, maybe, the wide cheekbones of a Finn),
Long hair for Jennifer, oriental eyes
And her pleased look imaginative of Carlos
Beside her in his listening, she absorbed
Like Echo by Narcissus' wonderment.
His notes take up a pattern on the page
With numerals and letters, for exams,
To recollect and sort what should be said,
The teacher absent. So Boethius,
As from a place made luminous by pain,
Repeats of his Dame Wisdom why the wicked
Prosper over the innocent—the cause,
Unfeeling Fortune, not like the sympathetic
Porsche or 530i Carlos imagined
But, on a twisting ball, her dark robe tattered
By hope and fear, a woman. How she fills
His mind with the old moon's pale bitterness
And how he grieves for mutability's
Expunging from the cosmos even him!

Quickly now, turn your Carlos to the window.
There, on the autumn green beyond the gym,
He sees blue girls and boys playing a game
His father played in Stockholm or Copenhagen
Within the high day luminous and still—
Moving, as if spontaneous, through his mind
Familiar with the day's small echoings.
And Jennifer? Her prudence is of him,
Remembering their soft kisses and the minor
New tendernesses taught by the desire
Some say once ruled the planets and the stars.

Chaco Canyon

Plato, my lord, might wonder, if he saw,
As we saw, from the cliff, the holy city
Built like a cave, its front shaped to the arc
The East's bright arrow follows in its flight.
And there, within, since daylight heat and glare
Are freshened by no breeze like the one that shoreward
Accompanies your mother on her shell,
Its people waited, fearful, for a brightness
Down from the mountain, in a violence
Of dark drums and of torches, suddenly
Out of an earth unburdened of its gift.
But then he might recall its wise men, watching
Silently, each new solstice, for the sun's
Quick step upon the mark high on the butte
Or, under unborn night, observing midnight
Against a cloud of stars and shooting stars
By Mercury's approach to Mars, as we
Observed the night before, a satellite
Conjured by his enraptured new disciples
Wavering across the axis out of sight.
Eleusis, Athens and Delos! Consciences
Alive, in the particulars of place!

The moon shone full and whiter than the dawn,
My lord. Along the cliff, the stony lichen
Seemed kin to the snake that Christopher awakened
From sleeping in the torpor spirits share;
While, fastened to the rock, the lunar flowers
That open in the dark gave off a scent,
When we stooped low to smell them, as of fields
Transcendent, where the blessed spirits gaze
Long on the smooth bright tables of desire
Expressive of the fortunes you prepare.
Along the path, under a meager growth
Of creosote and scattered in the powdery

Grey laval dust, were sherds, angled design
From some old common syntax of the mind;
And, on a wrinkled tree trunk near the fort
That overlooks the washes to the north,
Two lizards, male and female. Steven and Christian,
Red hair and black, almost thirteen and twelve,
Embarrassed, fascinated, boyishly obscene,
Kneeled to behold the prehistoric trance
Of roseate pale bodies pressed together,
Bellies moon-white and green and visions fixed
On rituals mysterious as air,
Hesitant, ardent, indifferent, all at once.
I thought of you, on Bacchus' arm, asleep.
Back in the valley, hot, in high noon's heat,
We played, too boisterous, under artesian streams
As fresh and cold as happiness, and soon
Were reprimanded by a uniform.

Later that night, around the fire, we two,
Happy again in our new dialogue
With you and Plato, heard Christian and Steven call
Their names from where they scrambled on the hill,
Until they met a girl in the next campground.
They moped back severe, furious with each other
And hating her, tormented, Christian threatening
To kill her the next day and, from his bed,
Cursing his friend, his enemy, his rival.
After breakfast, they climbed the hill again,
Challenging all the campground with their cries,
Tarzans, without a need or care for Jane.

If I have ever pleased you, give me, this once,
Unspirited by what has happened since,
To see distinct and honestly the truth
Of our adventure, not as Georgia O'Keeffe
Collected from the moon-dry sand a skull
As final as a piece of broken light
For her mimesis, but with such circumstance

As Plato keeps vivacious for his memoir
And such light as in oaks above Jalama
Is part shade and reflections of the shade.

We stopped, on our way back, to try the springs
At Ojo Caliente. Naked, we entered
Slowly, with short sharp cries of pain and pleasure,
An iron water hotter than human blood
And drank the slow pulse hot from the mineral vein.
Dizzy with heat, maybe hallucinated
By smelling the jimson flower back on the cliff,
Time shrunk into a white cloud far away,
I thought I had received the gift of tongues
And called out in the murk, "I have a vision
Requiring me to tell why all things are.
In the undark untime, long before *Don Giovanni*
And the *B Minor Mass* were natures, the moon
Fell for the sun. Round and round the abyss
She chased him, till desire was so intense
That, from its center, through the gathering blue,
A youth appeared. When, past the seas of crisis
And the deep lake of dreams, he reached the small
Sea of tranquility, then, on its bed,
They knew such joy that the one became the many
Divided and distributed in time
And every habitation of the seas
Of air and earth and water, as a fire.
You are the fire, my lord: your quickening step,
Your ankle curved up sweetly to the calf,
Your ass cheeks poised together for your stride
Proud beneath the body's pathos, your arms
Triumphant and throat smoother than the dove's,
Your face divine, from whose smile comes the tender
Intimate voice, the body's echo, and
Your hair, still brushed by traces of the sun."

Steven and Christian jeered, though, as boys are,
Made reckless by exuberance. Christopher,

Though pleased to know I took him for a model,
Upon the cruel mirror offered him
Saw, opening his pale wing, your younger twin
Haunt love and beauty with old age and death;
And, feeling that embrace within the car
To Santa Fe, heard his new sorrow sung,
As if without redemption, in one man's
"*Ach, kennst du nicht dein Kind?*" played on a tape.
The highway seemed the future. Steven and Christian
Stirred in their sleep, exhausted. Night wore by.
Though Plato's eyes were open, in a dream
Remembering the canyon, he foresaw
That, in the time to come, a man, encamped
For years beside a ruin once a city
Exposed to the indifference of the sun
And moon, inquiring of the breathless dust
That covers all things made of it, one day,
Among the ashes, bones and sherds, will find
Preserved by an egyptian air a memoir,
And, bringing it to the light, will read of us,
Dazzled by time and by what time provides.

In Defense of Poetry

Childhood taught us illusion. When I saw
On Frederick March's hands the fierce black hair
And long sharp nails of Mr. Hyde, I ran
Screaming from the theater, his twisted face
Demonic behind me brighter than the day;
Then begged to stay up past bedtime, for fear
Boris Karloff wake me and, near despair,
I run to consolation through the dark.
And while Miss Hinton taught us spelling, grammar,
Multiplication—all like loving guides
To bring us safely from the labyrinth
Of self and self's intelligence—it seemed
I heard the voice that mocked them. "There is no
Language," it whispered, "no A on tests, no trust
To keep you from the presence of my face.
Parents and children die, anguish will be
Greater than its hard sum and no familiar
Voices deliver you from Mr. Hyde,
However Dr. Jekyll seem secure."

Now in a bright room in a building named
For one who taught the art of politics,
Three days a week I listen to the stories
My young friends write, remembering that my father
Loved stories and especially those he told.
Intelligent and brave, they risk their way
By speech from childhood anguish, formal candor
An old light shining new within a world
Confusing and confused, although their teachers
Deny the worth of writing—my latest colleagues,
Who hope to find a letter in the mail,
Are happy if their children study Shakespeare
At Harvard, Penn or Yale, write articles
To prove all writing writers' self-deception,
Drive Camrys, drink good wines, play Shostakovich

Or TV news before they go to bed,
And when their sleeping or their waking dream
Is fearful, think it merely cinema,
Trite spectacle that later will amuse.
But when my mind remembers, unamused
It pictures Korczak going with his children
Through Warsaw to the too substantial train.

Princeton Series of Contemporary Poets